God's POWER in Your LIFE

Other books by
R. A. TORREY

The Bible Answer Book

Difficulties in the Bible

God, the Bible, and You

How to Bring Men to Christ

How to Pray

How to Study the Bible

How to Witness to Anyone

Power-Filled Living

Prayer and Faith

What the Bible Teaches

God's
POWER
in Your LIFE

R.A. TORREY

WHITAKER
HOUSE

Publisher's note:
This new edition from Whitaker House has been updated for
the modern reader. Words, expressions, and sentence structure
have been revised for clarity and readability.

All Scripture quotations are taken from the
King James Version of the Holy Bible.

GOD'S POWER IN YOUR LIFE
(Previously published as *How to Obtain Fullness of Power*)

ISBN-13: 978-088368-862-5 • ISBN-10: 0-88368-862-X
Printed in the United States of America
© 1982 by Whitaker House

Whitaker House
1030 Hunt Valley Circle
New Kensington, PA 15068
website: www.whitakerhouse.com

Library of Congress Cataloging-in-Publication Data

Torrey, R. A. (Reuben Archer), 1856–1928.
  God's power in your life / by R.A. Torrey.
    p. cm.
  Rev. ed. of: How to obtain fullness of power.
  Summary: "An examination of the power of God in the Christian life
as revealed in the Bible and as experienced through prayer"
—Provided by publisher.
  ISBN-10: 0-88368-862-X (trade pbk. : alk. paper)
  ISBN-13: 978-0-88368-862-5 (trade pbk. : alk. paper) 1. Christian
life—Biblical teaching. I. Torrey, R. A. (Reuben Archer), 1856–1928.
How to obtain fullness of power. II. Title.
  BS680.C47T67 2005
  248.4—dc22
                          2004028294

2 3 4 5 6 7 8 9 10 11 **UJ** 17 16 15 14 13 12 11

Contents

Preface

Preface

A cry for more power in our personal conflict with the world, the flesh, and the Devil is rising from many earnest hearts; also, there is a need for more power in our service to others. The Bible makes it very clear how to obtain this greatly desired power. There is no presumption in undertaking to tell how to obtain fullness of power in Christian life and service. The Bible itself tells how, and the Bible was intended to be understood.

The Bible's statement of the way to experience power is not mystical or mysterious; it is very plain and straightforward. If we will only practice personally the power of the Word of God, the power of the blood of Christ, the power of the Holy Spirit, the power of prayer, and the power of a surrendered life, we will then experience the fullness of power in Christian life and service. The following chapters make this clear.

The present volume has been written partly in response to a request from readers of the author's book *How to Bring Men to Christ,** suggesting a follow-up book for use in the training of those who have just accepted Christ. But this book has another and far more important purpose. Many do not even know that there is a life of abiding rest, joy, satisfaction, and power in Jesus. Many others, while they think there must be something beyond the life they know, are in ignorance as to how to obtain it. This book is written to help them.

---

* Available from Whitaker House.

Chapter 1
The Power of
the Word of God

one

The Power of the Word of God

The power that belongs to God is stored in the great reservoir of His own Word, the Bible. *"Power belongeth unto God"* (Psalm 62:11). If we wish to make it ours, we must go to the Bible. Yet people who pray for power but neglect the Bible abound in the church.

Many long to have power for fruit-bearing in their own lives, yet they forget that Jesus has said, *"The seed is the word of God"* (Luke 8:11). They long to have power to melt the cold heart and break the stubborn will, yet they forget that God has said, *"Is not my word like as a fire?... and like a hammer that breaketh the rock in pieces?"* (Jeremiah 23:29).

If we are to obtain fullness of power in life and service, we must feed on the Word of God.

No other food is so strengthening. If we will not take time to study the Bible, we cannot have power anymore than we can have physical strength if we will not take time to eat nutritious food. Let us see what the Word of God has the power to do.

Conviction of Sin

First of all, the Word of God has the power to convict of sin. In Acts 2:37, we read, *"Now when they heard this, they were pricked in their heart, and said unto Peter and to the rest of the apostles, Men and brethren, what shall we do?"* If we look to see what they heard that produced this deep conviction, we find that it was simply the Word of God.

We must feed on the Word of God.

If we will read Peter's sermon, we will find it to be one of the most biblical sermons ever preached. It was Scripture from beginning to end. It was the Word of God, carried home by the Spirit of God, that pricked their minds and hearts.

If we wish to produce conviction, we must give people the Word of God. Once, I heard a man pray this prayer, "O God, convict us of sin." That was a very good prayer, but unless we bring our souls into contact with the instrument God designed for the conviction

14

of sin, we will feel nothing. And if we desire to produce conviction in others, we must use the Word.

The Greatest Sin

Not long ago, a fine-looking young man came up to me after a meeting. I asked him, "Are you a Christian?"

He answered, "No, sir."

"Why not?"

"I think Christianity is a first-rate thing, but I don't have much feeling about it."

"But," I said, "do you realize that you are a sinner?"

He said, "Yes, sir, I suppose I am, but I am not very much of a sinner. I am a pretty good sort of fellow."

"So, my friend, you do not have very much conviction of sin. I have something in my hand that is a divinely appointed instrument to produce conviction of sin." Opening my Bible, I asked him to read Matthew 22:37–38.

He read, *"Thou shalt love the Lord thy God with all thy heart, and with all thy soul, and with all thy mind. This is the first and great commandment."*

Then I asked him, "In light of this Scripture, what is the first and greatest sin?"

He replied, "It must be to neglect to keep that commandment."

"Have you kept it?" I asked. At this point, the Spirit of God took it home to his heart. Not long after that, we were kneeling as he asked God for mercy through Christ.

Life-Giving Power

The Word of God has the power to regenerate. In 1 Peter 1:23, we read, *"Being born again, not of corruptible seed, but of incorruptible, by the word of God, which liveth and abideth for ever."* James 1:18 says, *"Of his own will begat he us with the word of truth, that we should be a kind of firstfruits of his creatures."*

If you wish to be born again, the way is very simple. Take the Word of God concerning Christ crucified and risen, and store it in your heart by meditating on it. Look to God to quicken it by His Holy Spirit. Believe it with your heart, and the work will be done.

The Word of God has power to regenerate.

If you wish to see someone else born again, give him the Word of God. Although God's part in the process of regeneration is a mystery to us, our part is quite simple: The human heart is the soil; you and I are sowers; the Word of

God is the seed that we plant in that soil; God quickens it by His Holy Spirit and gives the increase (1 Corinthians 3:6); the heart closes around the Word by faith; and the new life is the product.

The new birth is simply the impartation of a new nature—God's nature. But how are we made partakers of God's nature? Read 2 Peter 1:4: *"That by these ['exceeding great and precious promises'] ye might be partakers of the divine nature."* That is all there is to it.

The Word of God is the seed out of which the divine nature springs up in the human soul.

Saving Faith

The Word of God also has the power to produce faith. In Romans 10:17, we read, *"Faith cometh by hearing, and hearing by the word of God."* You can never get faith by merely praying. You can never get it by an effort of the will. You can never get it by trying to "pump it up" in any way. Faith is the effect of a certain cause, and that cause is the Word of God.

Such is the case, for example, with saving faith. Suppose you want a man to have saving faith. Simply give him something definite from God's Word on which he can rest. The Philippian jailer asked, *"Sirs, what must I do to be saved?"* (Acts 16:30), and Paul and Silas answered, *"Believe on* the Lord Jesus Christ, and thou shalt be saved, and thy house" (Acts 16:31).

But they did not stop there. Read verse 32: "And they spake unto him the word of the Lord, and to all that were in his house." They did not merely tell the Philippian jailer to believe in the Lord Jesus Christ and then leave him there floundering in the dark without giving him something to believe or something to rest his faith upon. They gave him what God has ordained to produce faith.

It is at this point that we often make a mistake. We tell people, "Believe, believe, believe," but do not show them how or give them anything definite to believe. The biblical way, and the intelligent way as well, is to tell a person to believe and then give him something to believe in. Give him, for example, Isaiah 53:6, and thus hold up Christ crucified, or give him 1 Peter 2:24. Here he has something for his faith to rest on. Faith must have a foundation; it cannot float in thin air. It is disheartening to see people told to believe when they are not given anything in which to believe.

> **Faith needs a foundation; it cannot float in thin air.**

Prevailing Faith

Not only does saving faith come through the Word of God, but also prevailing faith in prayer. Suppose I read Mark 11:24: "What things soever ye *desire, when ye pray, believe that ye receive them, and ye shall have them.*" I used to say, "The way to get anything I want is to believe I am going to get it." I would kneel down and pray, trying to believe, but I did not get the things that I asked for. I had no real faith.

Real faith must have a guarantee. Before I can truly believe I am to receive what I ask for, I must have a definite promise from God's Word or a definite leading of the Holy Spirit to rest my faith on. What, then, should we do?

We go into God's presence with the thing we desire. Next, we ask ourselves this question: Is there any promise in God's Word regarding what I desire? We look into the Word of God and find the promise. Then all we have to do is to present that promise to God. For example, we say, "Heavenly Father, I desire the Holy Spirit. You say in Your Word, '*If ye then, being evil, know how to give good gifts unto your children: how much more shall your heavenly Father give the Holy Spirit to them that ask him?*' (Luke 11:13). And again in Acts 2:39, You say that '*the promise is unto you, and to your children, and to all that are afar off, even as many as the Lord our God shall call.*' I have been called; I am saved; and here in Your Word is Your promise. So please fill me now with the Holy Spirit."

We then take 1 John 5:14–15 and say, "Father, I have confidence in You that if I ask anything according to Your will—and I know that this petition is according to Your will—You hear me. And since I know that You hear me, I know that I have the request that I have asked of You."

Then we stand on God's promise and say, "It is mine," and it will be. The only way to have a faith that prevails in prayer is to study your Bible, know the promises, and present them to God. George Müller, one of the church's mightiest men of prayer, always prepared for prayer by studying the Word.

Christian Evidence

The Word of God also gives us the faith we need to dispel doubt. Suppose you have a skeptic to deal with, and you desire that he will receive faith. What will you do with him? To begin with, turn to John 20:31: *"But these are written, that ye might believe that Jesus is the Christ, the Son of God; and that believing ye might have life through his name."* Clearly, then, this book of John was given that through *"those things which are written therein"* (Revelation 1:3), men *"might believe that Jesus is the Christ, the Son of God; and that believing [they] might have life through his name"* (John 20:31). The gospel of John is an inspired book on Christian evidence.

Then, find out whether the skeptic's will is surrendered or not. *"If any man will do his will, he shall know of the doctrine, whether it be of God, or whether I speak of myself"* (John 7:17). After the will has been surrendered, just say, "Take this Book and read it thoughtfully and honestly. Then come back and tell me the result." The result is absolutely sure.

No person—agnostic, infidel, or whatever you please—can read the Bible, asking the Holy Spirit to give him light, without coming to believe in Jesus as the Christ, the Son of God—provided that his will is surrendered to the truth. I have tried this with many men and women, and there has never been one exception to the rule laid down by Christ. It has always come out the same way.

Faith wins victories through the Word.

Victorious Faith

Faith that wins mighty victories for God—that gets the victory over the world, the flesh, and the Devil—comes through the Word. (See 1 John 5:4; Ephesians 6:16; Hebrews 11:33–34.) Very early in my ministry, I read a sermon by D. L. Moody in which he said that a man would not amount to anything if he did not have faith. I said, "That sermon is true. I must have faith." I went to work and tried to generate some faith, with no success. The more I tried, the less I had. But one day, I ran across this text: *"Faith cometh by hearing, and hearing by the word of God"* (Romans 10:17). In it, I learned the great secret of faith, one of the greatest secrets I have ever learned.

I began to feed my faith on the Word of God, and it has been growing ever since. So, in every respect, we see that *"faith cometh by hearing, and hearing by the word of God."* If we are to have faith, we must feed steadily, largely, and daily on the Word of God.

Cleansing

The Word of God has the power to cleanse. In Ephesians 5:25–26, we read, *"Husbands, love your wives, even as Christ also loved the church, and gave himself for it; that he might sanctify and cleanse it with the washing of water by the word."* The Word of God has the power not only to take impurities out of the heart but also to cleanse the outward life as well. If you want a clean outward life, you must wash it often by bringing your life into contact with the Word of God.

If one lives in a city whose atmosphere is polluted with smoke, his hands will get black when he goes into the street. He must wash frequently if he wishes to keep clean. We all live in a very dirty world whose spiritual atmosphere is polluted. As we go out from day to day, coming into contact with it, there is only one way to keep clean: by taking frequent baths in the Word of God. You must bathe every day and take plenty of time to do it. A daily, prolonged, thoughtful bath in the Word of God is the only thing that will keep a life clean. (See Psalm 119:9.)

The Word of God has the power to build up.

Character Building

The Word of God has the power to build up. In Acts 20:32, we read, *"I commend you to God, and to the word of his grace, which is able to build you up."* Character building should be done according to the Word of God. In 2 Peter 1:5–7, we have a picture of a seven-story Christian built on the foundation of faith. The great trouble today is that we have too many one-story Christians because of their neglect of the Word.

In 1 Peter 2:2, we have a similar thought expressed in a different way: *"As newborn babes, desire the pure milk of the word, that ye may grow thereby."* If we are to grow, we must have wholesome, nutritious food and plenty of it.

The only spiritual food that contains all the elements necessary for balanced Christian growth is the Word of God. A Christian can no more grow up in good health without feeding frequently, regularly, and largely on the Word of God than a baby can grow up in good health without proper nutrition.

Wisdom

The Word of God has the power to give wisdom. Psalm 119:130 is worthy of the most careful attention: *"The entrance of thy words giveth light; it giveth understanding unto the simple."* There is more wisdom in the Bible than there is in all the other literature of the ages. The man who studies the Bible, even if he does not study any other book, will possess more real wisdom—wisdom that counts for eternity as well as time, wisdom that this perishing world needs, wisdom for which hungry hearts today are starving—than the man who reads every other book and neglects his Bible.

The Word has more wisdom than all literature.

This has been illustrated over and over again in the history of the church. Men who have greatly affected the spiritual history of this world, those who have brought about great reformations in morals and doctrines, men whom others have flocked to hear and on whose words people have hung, have been men of the Bible in every instance. In many cases, they knew little besides the Bible.

The Power of the Word of God

I have known unsophisticated men and women who knew little more than their Bibles. I would rather sit at their feet and learn the wisdom that falls from their lips than listen to the man well-versed in philosophy, science, and even theology if he does not know anything about the Word of God. There is wonderful force in the words of Paul to Timothy:

> *All scripture is given by inspiration of God, and is profitable for doctrine, for reproof, for correction, for instruction in righteousness: that the man of God may be perfect, thoroughly furnished unto all good works.* (2 Timothy 3:16–17)

Through what? Through the study of the Bible.

Eternal Life

The Word of God has the power to give assurance of eternal life. In 1 John 5:13, we read, *"These things have I written unto you that believe on the name of the Son of God; that ye may know that ye have eternal life, and that ye may believe on the name of the Son of God."* That is, the assurance of eternal life comes through what is *"written."*

What should we do with someone who is not sure of his salvation? Tell him to pray until he gets assurance? Not at all. Instead, take him to a passage such as John 3:36: *"He that believeth on the Son hath everlasting life."* Make him focus on that point until he takes God's Word as truth and knows he has everlasting life because he believes on the Son and because God says, *"He that believeth on the Son hath everlasting life"* (John 3:36).

The Peace of the Lord

The Word of God has the power to bring peace into the heart. In Psalm 85:8, we read, *"I will hear what God the LORD will speak: for he will speak peace unto his people, and to his saints."* Many people today are looking for peace, longing for peace, and praying for peace. But deep peace of heart comes only from the study of the Word of God.

There is, for example, one passage in the Bible that, if fed on daily until it becomes indelibly written on our hearts, will banish all anxiety forever. It is Romans 8:28: *"And we know that all things work together for good to them that love God, to them who are the called according to his purpose."* Nothing can come to us that is not one of the *"all things."* If we really believe this passage and it really takes hold of us, nothing will disturb our peace.

Joy! Joy! Joy!

The Word of God has the power to produce joy. Jeremiah 15:16 says, *"Thy words were found, and I did eat them; and thy word was unto me the joy and rejoicing of mine heart."* And Jesus said in John 15:11, *"These things have I spoken unto you, that my joy might remain in you, and that your joy might be full."* Clearly, then, fullness of joy comes through the Word of God.

There is no joy on this earth, from any worldly source, like the joy that kindles and glows in the heart of a believer in Jesus Christ. This joy comes as he feeds on the Word of God and as the Word of God is engraved on his heart by the power of the Holy Spirit.

Patience, comfort, and hope also come through the Word of God. Romans 15:4 says, *"For whatsoever things were written aforetime were written for our learning, that we through patience and comfort of the scriptures might have hope."*

The Power to Protect

Finally, the Word of God has the power to protect us from error and sin. In Acts 20:29–32, the apostle Paul warned the elders at Ephesus of the errors that would creep in among them. He commended them, in closing, *"to God, and to the word of his grace"* (verse 32). In a similar way, Paul, writing to Timothy, the bishop of the same church, said,

Fullness of joy comes through the Word.

> *But evil men and seducers shall wax worse and worse, deceiving, and being deceived. But continue thou in the things which thou hast learned and*

hast been assured of, knowing of whom thou hast learned them; and that from a child thou hast known the holy scriptures, which are able to make thee wise unto salvation through faith which is in Christ Jesus. (2 Timothy 3:13–15)

The one who feeds constantly on the Word of God is protected from committing errors. It is simple neglect of the Word that has left so many believers prey to the many false doctrines with which the Devil, in his subtlety, is endeavoring to infiltrate the church of Christ today.

The Word of God not only has the power to protect from error but from sin as well. In Psalm 119:11, we read, *"Thy word have I hid in mine heart, that I might not sin against thee."* The man who feeds daily on the Word of God will be protected against the temptations of the Devil. Any day we neglect to feed on the Word of God, we leave an open door through which Satan is sure to enter our hearts and lives. Even the Son of God Himself met and overcame the temptations of the Adversary by the Scriptures. To each of Satan's temptations, Jesus replied, *"It is written"* (Matthew 4:4, 7, 10). Satan left the field completely vanquished.

Study the Word

It is evident from what has been said that the first step in obtaining fullness of power in Christian life and service is the study of the

Word. There can be no fullness of power in life and service if the Bible is neglected. In much that is now written on power, this fact is overlooked. The work of the Holy Spirit is magnified, but the instrument through which the Holy Spirit works is largely forgotten. The result is transient enthusiasm and activity but no steady continuance and increase in power and usefulness.

We cannot obtain or maintain power in our own lives or in our work for others unless there is deep and frequent meditation on the Word of God. If our leaf is not to wither and if whatever we do is to prosper, our delight must be in the law of the Lord, and we must meditate on it day and night (Psalm 1:2–3).

Our delight should be in the law of the Lord.

Of course, it is much easier and more agreeable to our spiritual laziness to go to a revival meeting claiming a "filling with the Holy Spirit" than it is to inch along day after day, month after month, year after year, digging into the Word of God. But a filling with the Spirit that is not maintained by persistent study of the Word will soon vanish. Precisely the same results that Paul in one place ascribed to being *"filled with the Spirit"* (Ephesians 5:18), in another place he attributed to letting *"the word of Christ dwell in you richly"* (Colossians 3:16). Evidently Paul knew of no filling with the Holy Spirit divorced from deep and constant meditation on the Word. To sum it all up, anyone who wishes to obtain and maintain fullness of power in Christian life and service must feed constantly on the Word of God.

Chapter 2
The Power of
the Blood of Christ

two

The Power of the Blood of Christ

Because *"power belongeth unto God"* (Psalm 62:11), it is at man's disposal. But there is one thing that separates man and God, and that is sin. We read in Isaiah,

Behold, the LORD'S hand is not shortened, that it cannot save; neither his ear heavy, that it cannot hear: but your iniquities have separated between you and your God, and your sins have hid his face from you, that he will not hear.

(Isaiah 59:1–2)

Before we can know God's power in our lives and service, sin must be removed in order to get rid of the separation between God and us.

It is Christ's blood that removes sin. (See Hebrews 9:26.) We must know the power of the blood if we are to know the power of God. Our experience of the power of the Word, the power of the Holy Spirit, and the power of prayer is dependent on our knowing the power of the blood of Christ. Let us see what the blood of Christ has the power to do.

Christ's Atoning Sacrifice

First of all, the blood of Christ is an offering to God for sin. In Romans 3:25, we read,

We must feed on the Word of God.

"Whom God hath set forth to be a propitiation through faith in his blood, to declare his righteousness for the remission of sins that are past, through the forbearance of God." In the earlier verses of this chapter, Paul proved all men to be sinners—*"that every mouth may be stopped, and all the world may become guilty before God"* (verse 19).

But God is holy, a God who hates sin. God's hatred of sin is no false hatred. It is real; it is living; it is active. Somehow, it must manifest itself. God's wrath at sin must strike somewhere. What hope then is there for any of us, for *"all have sinned, and come short of the glory of God"* (verse 23)?

The Blood of Jesus

God gives us His own answer to this tremendously important question. There is hope for us because God Himself has provided an appeasement: the shed blood of Christ. God has *"set forth* [Christ] *to be a propitiation through faith in his blood"* (verse 25). The wrath of God at sin strikes Christ instead of striking us.

The prophet Isaiah glimpsed this great truth several hundred years before the birth of Christ. *"All we like sheep have gone astray; we have turned every one to his own way; and the LORD hath laid* [literally, made to strike] *on him the iniquity of us all"* (Isaiah 53:6).

The first power of Christ's blood is as a sin offering, providing a target for and satisfying God's holy wrath at sin. He is *"our passover"* (1 Corinthians 5:7). When God sees His blood, He will pass over and spare us, even though we are sinners. (See Exodus 12:13, 23.)

This propitiation is chiefly for the believer, *"a propitiation through faith"* (Romans 3:25). All of God's wrath at the believer's sins is fully appeased or satisfied in the blood of Christ. What a wonderfully comforting thought it is when we remember how often and how greatly we have sinned, to know how infinitely holy God is, how He hates sin, and how His wrath

There is hope because of Christ's shed blood.

has already been fully appeased in the shed blood of His own Son, the propitiation that He Himself provided!

35

Believers and Unbelievers

The blood of Christ covers unbelievers as well as believers, the vilest sinner and the most stubborn unbeliever and blasphemer. In 1 John 2:2, we read, *"And he is the propitiation for our sins: and not for ours only, but also for the sins of the whole world."* By the shed blood of Christ, a basis is provided on which God can deal mercifully with the whole world.

All of God's dealings in mercy with man are on the ground of the shed blood of Christ. And more, His dealings with those who ridicule the doctrine of the Atonement are on the ground of that shed blood. All the mercy of God on man since the fall of Adam is on the ground of that shed blood. Without the shed blood, God would cut the sinner off at once in his sin.

Someone may ask, "How then could God have dealt in mercy with sinners before Christ came and died?" The answer is simple. Jesus is the Lamb who was *"slain from the foundation of the world"* (Revelation 13:8).

From the moment sin entered the world, God had His eyes on that sacrifice that He Himself had prepared *"from the foundation of the world."* In the very garden of Eden, the blood of sacrifices that pointed to the true sacrifice began to flow. It is the power of the blood that has given men the security of God's mercy since sin arrived.

The Power of the Blood of Christ

The most determined rejecter of Christ owes all he has that is good to Christ's blood.

Forgiveness

Again, in Ephesians 1:7, we read, *"We have redemption through his blood, the forgiveness of sins."* Forgiveness of sins is not something the believer in Christ is to look for in the future; it is something he already has. *"We have,"* said Paul, *"...the forgiveness of* [our] *sins."*

Forgiveness of sin is not something we are to do; it is not something to secure. It is something that the blood of Christ has already secured, which our faith simply appropriates and enjoys. Forgiveness has already been secured for every believer in Christ by the power of His blood. Oh, blessed is the one who has learned to rest in the peace Christ gives, who counts his sins forgiven because Christ's blood was shed and God says so! *"We have redemption through his blood, the forgiveness of sins."*

> **Blessed is he who rests in Christ's peace!**

Continuous Cleansing

Another passage very closely related to this one reveals the power of Christ's blood even further: *"But if we walk in the light, as he is in the light, we have fellowship one with another, and the blood of Jesus Christ his Son cleanseth us from all sin*" (1 John 1:7). This describes the completeness of the forgiveness we get through the blood. The blood of Christ has the power to cleanse the believer from *"all sin."* And it cleanses continuously, keeping him clean every minute, every day, and every hour.

The cleansing here is from the guilt of sin. When cleansing is mentioned in the Bible in connection with the blood, it is always cleansing from guilt. Cleansing from the power of sin and the presence of sin is by the Word of God, the Holy Spirit, and the living and indwelling Christ. Christ on the cross saves from the guilt of sin; Christ on the throne saves from the power of sin; and Christ coming again will save from the presence of sin.

White as Snow

When one is walking in the light, submitting to the light, and walking in Christ who is the Light, then the blood of Christ cleanses from *all* the guilt of sin. His past may be as bad as a past can be, laden with countless, enormous sins, but they are all—every one, the greatest and the smallest—washed away. His record is absolutely white in God's sight. It is as white as the record of Jesus Christ Himself. His sins that were as scarlet are as white as snow; though they were red like crimson, they are as wool. (See Isaiah 1:18.)

The Power of the Blood of Christ

The blood of Christ has the power to wash the blackest record white. We all have had black pasts, for if we could see our pasts as God sees them before they are washed, the records of the best of us would be black, black, black. But if we are walking in the light, submitting to the truth of God, believing in the light—in Christ—our records today are as white as Christ's garments were when the disciples saw Him on the Mount of Transfiguration. (See Matthew 17:2; Mark 9:3; Luke 9:29.) No one can lay anything to the charge of God's elect (Romans 8:33); there is no condemnation to those who are in Christ Jesus (Romans 8:1).

The blood of Christ cleanses continuously.

Saved from Wrath

In Romans 5:9, we read, *"Much more then, being now justified by his blood, we shall be saved from wrath through him."* The blood of Christ has the power to justify. Every believer in Christ is already justified in Christ's blood. This means that he is more than forgiven and cleansed.

Forgiveness, as glorious as it is, is a negative thing. It means merely that our sins are put away, and we are regarded as if we had not sinned. But justification is positive. It means that we are counted as positively righteous, that positive and perfect righteousness—the perfect righteousness of Christ—is credited to our account.

It is a good thing to be stripped of vile and filthy rags, but it is far better to be clothed with garments of glory and beauty. In forgiveness, we are stripped of the vile and stinking rags of our sin. In justification, we are clothed with the glory and beauty of Christ. The power of the blood secures this experience.

In shedding His blood as a penalty for sin, Christ took our place; when we believe in Him, we step into His place. *"For he hath made him to be sin for us, who knew no sin; that we might be made the righteousness of God in him"* (2 Corinthians 5:21).

No More Dead Works

Now let us look at Hebrews 9:14: *"How much more shall the blood of Christ, who through the eternal Spirit offered himself without spot to God, purge your conscience from dead works to serve the living God?"* The blood of Christ has the power to cleanse the conscience from dead works to serve the living God. Do you understand what that means? It is a glorious truth, and I will try to make it plain.

When a man awakens to the fact that he is a sinner and that God is holy, he feels that he must do something to please God and atone for sin. He must somehow make restitution or give away money to atone for his sins. All these self-efforts to please God and atone for sins are *"dead works."* They can never accomplish what they aim at and can never bring peace. For many weary years, Martin Luther sought peace in this way and did not find it. But when we see, as Luther finally did, how the power of the blood washed away our sins and justified us before God, making us pleasing and acceptable in God's sight by reason of that shed blood, then our consciences are not only relieved from the burden of guilt but also from the burden of our self-efforts. We are now at liberty to serve the living God—not in the slavery of fear, but in the liberty of the freedom and joy of those who know they are accepted and beloved sons.

Self-efforts to please God are *"dead works."*

It is the blood that delivers us from the awful bondage of thinking we must do something to atone for sins and please God. The blood shows us that it is already done.

Do or Done?

A friend of mine once said to someone who was seeking peace through his own works, "You have a two-letter religion, and I have a four-letter one."

"How is that?" asked the other man.

"Your religion is *do*. My religion is *done*. You are trying to rest in what you do. I am resting in what Christ has done."

Many Christians today have not permitted the blood of Christ to cleanse their consciences from dead works. They are constantly feeling they must do something to atone for sin. Look at what God looks at—the blood—and see that it is already done! God is satisfied; sin is atoned for; you are justified! Don't do *"dead works"* to commend yourself to God. Realize that you are already commended by the blood; then serve Him in the freedom of love, not in the bondage of fear.

Many still feel they must atone for sin.

There are three kinds of men. First, there are those who are not at all burdened by sin, who, on the contrary, love it. That is wholly bad. Second, there are those who are burdened by sin and seek to get rid of it by their own works. That is better, but there is something infinitely better. Third, there are those who saw the hideousness of sin and were burdened by it but who have been brought to see the power of the blood, settling sin forever and putting it away (Hebrews 9:26). They are no longer burdened and no longer work to commend themselves to God. Rather, out of joyous gratitude, they serve Him who perfectly justifies the ungodly through His shed blood.

God's Own

In Acts 20:28, we read,

Take heed therefore unto yourselves, and to all the flock, over the which the Holy Ghost hath made you overseers, to feed the church of God, which he hath purchased with his own blood.

Revelation 5:9 says,

And they sung a new song, saying, Thou art worthy to take the book, and to open the seals thereof: for thou wast slain, and hast redeemed us to God by thy blood out of every kindred, and tongue, and people, and nation.

The blood of Christ has the power to purchase us, to make us God's own. The blood of Christ makes me God's own property.

That thought brings me a feeling of responsibility. If I belong to God, I must serve Him wholly; body, soul, and spirit must be surrendered completely to Him. But the thought that I am God's property also brings a feeling of security. God can and will take care of His own property. The blood of Christ has power to make me eternally secure.

The blood of Christ has the power to purchase us.

Holy Boldness

We learn still more about the power of the blood in Hebrews 10:19–20: *"Therefore, brethren,* [we have] *boldness to enter the holiest by the blood of Jesus, by a new and living way, which he hath consecrated for us, through the veil, that is to say, his flesh."* The blood of Christ has the power to give the believer boldness to enter into the Holy Place, the very presence of God.

In the old Jewish days of the tabernacle and temple, God manifested Himself in the Most Holy Place. This was the place to meet God. Only one Jew in all the nation was allowed to enter this hallowed place—the high priest. He could go in only once a year, on the Day of Atonement, and then only with blood.

God was teaching the Jews—and through them, the world—three great truths: that God is unapproachably holy, that man is sinful, and that sinful man can approach a holy God only through atoning blood. That is, *"without shedding of blood is no remission"* of sin (Hebrews 9:22) and, consequently, no approach to God.

But the blood of the Old Testament sacrifices was only a symbol of the true sacrifice, Jesus Christ. Because of His shed blood, the vilest sinner who believes on Him has the right to approach God boldly, going into His very presence, whenever he desires, without fear, *"in full assurance of faith"* (Hebrews 10:22).

The wondrous power of the blood of Christ removes all fear when I draw near to the *"consuming fire"* (Hebrews 12:29) of my most holy God. Yes, I am a sinner. But by that wondrous offering of Christ *"once"* (Hebrews 9:12), my sin is forever put away. I am *"perfected"* (Hebrews 10:14) and *"justified"* (Romans 3:24). On the ground of that blood so precious and satisfying to God, I can march boldly into the very presence of God.

The Tree of Life

But the blood of Christ has still further power. Read Revelation 22:14: *"Blessed are they that do his commandments, that they may have right to the tree of life, and may enter in through the gates into the city."* Then read Revelation 7:14: *"These are they which came out of great tribulation, and have washed their robes, and made them white in the blood of the Lamb."* We see that it is in the blood of Christ that robes are

We can march boldly into God's presence.

washed. The blood of Christ, therefore, has the power to give those who believe in Him a right to the Tree of Life and entrance into the city of God.

Sin shut men away from the Tree of Life and out of Eden. (See Genesis 3:22–24.) The shed blood of Christ reopens the way to the Tree of Life and to the New Jerusalem. The blood of Christ regains all that Adam lost by sin and brings us much more than what was lost.

We Need His Atoning Blood

Do you fully appreciate the blood of Christ? Have you let it have the power that it ought to have? Some today try to devise a theology that leaves out the blood of Christ.

Without the blood, there is no mercy.

But Christianity without the atoning blood is a Christianity without mercy for the sinner, without settled peace for the conscience, without genuine forgiveness, without justification, without cleansing, without boldness in approaching God—*without power.* It is not Christianity but the Devil's own counterfeit.

If we desire fullness of power in Christian life and service, we must know the power of the blood of Christ, for it is what brings us pardon, justification, and boldness in our approach to God. We cannot experience the power of the Spirit until we know the power of the blood. We certainly cannot experience the power of prayer until we know the power of that blood by which alone we can approach God.

Those who ignore the fundamental truth about the blood are trying to build a lofty superstructure without a firm foundation. It is bound to tumble. We must begin with the blood if we are to go on into the Holy of Holies. Every priest who entered the Holy Place first met the bronze altar where blood was shed. There is no other way of entrance there.

If we do not learn the lesson of this chapter, it is useless for us to try to learn the lessons of chapters three and four. To everyone who wishes to know the power of the Spirit, we first put this question: "Do you know the power of the blood?"

Chapter 3
The Power of the Holy Spirit

three

The Power of the Holy Spirit

T he Holy Spirit is the person who imparts to believers the power that *"belongeth unto God"* (Psalm 62:11). The Holy Spirit's work in believers is to take what belongs to God and make it theirs. All the manifold power of God belongs to the children of God as their birthright in Christ: *"For all things are yours"* (1 Corinthians 3:21). But all that belongs to believers as their birthright in Christ becomes theirs in actual possession through the Holy Spirit's work in them as individuals.

Claim the Spirit

We obtain the fullness of power that God has provided for us in Christ to the same extent that we understand and claim the Holy Spirit's work for ourselves. Many in the church claim for themselves only a small part of what God has made possible for them in Christ because they know so little of what the Holy Spirit can do—and longs to do—for us. To find out what the Holy Spirit has the power to do in men, let us study the Word of God.

We will not go far before we discover that the same work that we see ascribed in one place to the power of the Word **The Word of** is in other places credited to the **God is the** Holy Spirit. The explanation of **Holy Spirit's** this is simple. The Word of God **instrument.** is the instrument through which the Holy Spirit does His work. The Word of God is *"the sword of the Spirit"* (Ephesians 6:17).

The Word of God is also the seed the Spirit sows and quickens. (See Luke 8:11; 1 Peter 1:23.) The Word of God is the instrument of all the varied operations of the Holy Spirit (as seen in chapter 1). Therefore, if we wish the Holy Spirit to do His work in our hearts, we must study the Word. If we wish Him to do His work in the hearts of others, we must give them the Word.

The Sword of the Spirit
The Word will not do the work alone. The Spirit Himself must use the Word because

when He uses His own sword, its real strength, keenness, and power are manifested. God's work is accomplished by the Spirit through the Word.

The secret of effective Christian living is knowing the power of the Spirit through the Word. The secret of effective Christian service is using the Word in the power of the Spirit.

Some believers magnify the Spirit but neglect the Word. This will not do because fanaticism and groundless enthusiasm are the result. Others seek to magnify the Word but largely ignore the Spirit. This will not do either. It leads to dead orthodoxy and to truth without life and power. The true course is to recognize both the instrumental power of the Word through which the Holy Spirit works and the living, personal power of the Holy Spirit who acts through the Word.

But let us get directly to the consideration of our subject: What does the Holy Spirit have the power to do?

The Spirit Reveals Christ

Read 1 Corinthians 12:3: *"Wherefore I give you to understand, that no man speaking by the Spirit of God calleth Jesus accursed: and that no man can say that Jesus is the Lord, but by the Holy Ghost."* The Holy Spirit has the power to reveal Jesus

Christ and His glory to man. When Jesus spoke of the Spirit's coming, He said, *"But when the Comforter is come, whom I will send unto you from the Father, even the Spirit of truth, which proceedeth from the Father, he shall testify of me"* (John 15:26). It is only by His testimony that men will ever come to a true knowledge of Christ.

The Spirit has the power to reveal Christ.

You can send men to the Word to get knowledge of Christ, but it is only through the Holy Spirit's illumination of the Word that men can get a real, living knowledge of Christ. *"No man can say that Jesus is the Lord, but by the Holy Ghost"* (1 Corinthians 12:3).

For men to get a true knowledge of Jesus Christ so that they will believe in Him and be saved, seek the testimony of the Holy Spirit for them. Neither your testimony nor that of the Word alone will suffice, though it is your testimony or that of the Word that the Spirit uses.

The Spirit Bears Witness

Unless your testimony is illuminated by the Holy Spirit and He Himself testifies, they will not believe. It was not merely Peter's words about Christ that convinced the Jews at Pentecost. It was the Spirit Himself bearing witness. If you wish men to know the truth about Jesus, do not depend on your own powers of explanation and persuasion, but give yourself to the Holy Spirit and ask for His testimony.

If you desire to know Jesus with a true and living knowledge, seek the witness of the Spirit through the Word. Many people have correct doctrinal conceptions of Christ through studying the Word long before they have true, personal knowledge of Christ through the testimony of the living Spirit.

The Spirit Convicts of Sin

Now let us read John 16:8–11:

And when he is come, he will reprove the world of sin, and of righteousness, and of judgment: of sin, because they believe not on me; of righteousness, because I go to my Father, and ye see me no more; of judgment, because the prince of this world is judged.

The Holy Spirit has the power to convict the world of sin. This is closely connected with His power to reveal Jesus, for it is by showing Christ's glory and His righteousness that the Holy Spirit convicts us of sin, righteousness, and judgment. Note the sin of which the Holy Spirit convicts: *"of sin, because they believe not on me."* It was so at Pentecost, as we see in Acts 2:36–37. You can never convict any man of sin because that is the work of the Holy Spirit. You can reason and reason, but you will fail.

The Holy Spirit, however, can do it very quickly. Have you ever had the experience of wondering why, after showing a man passage after passage of Scripture, he remained unmoved? You were trying to convict the man of sin by yourself rather than looking, in your powerlessness, to the mighty Spirit of God to do it. When you let the Spirit of God do the work, conviction comes. The Spirit can convince the most indifferent person, as experience has proven again and again.

But it is through us that the Spirit produces conviction. In John 16:7–8, we read,

> *Nevertheless I tell you the truth; it is expedient for you that I go away: for if I go not away, the Comforter will not come unto you; but if I depart, I will send him unto you. And when he is come, he will reprove the world of sin, and of righteousness, and of judgment.*

It was the Spirit sent to Peter and the rest who convicted the three thousand on the day of Pentecost. (See Acts 2:4–37.) It is ours to preach the Word and to look to the Holy Spirit to produce conviction.

The Spirit Renews

In Titus 3:5, we read, *"Not by works of righteousness which we have done, but according to his mercy he saved us, by the washing of regeneration, and renewing of the Holy Ghost."*

The Power of the Holy Spirit

The Holy Spirit has the power to renew men. Regeneration is His work. He can take a man dead in trespasses and sins and make him alive. He can transform the man whose mind is blind to the truth of God, whose will is at enmity with God and set on sin, and whose affections are corrupt and vile. He imparts God's nature to him so that he thinks God's thoughts, wills what God wills, loves what God loves, and hates what God hates.

Regeneration is the work of the Holy Spirit.

I never lose hope for a man when I remember the regenerative power of the Holy Spirit, for I have seen it manifested again and again in the most hardened and hopeless cases. But it is through us that the Holy Spirit regenerates others. (See 1 Corinthians 4:15, for example.)

As we learned in chapter 1, the Word has the power to regenerate, but not on its own. It must be made a living thing in the heart by the power of the Holy Spirit. No amount of preaching and no amount of mere study of the Word will regenerate without the assistance of the Holy Spirit. Just as we are utterly dependent on the work of Christ for our justification, so we are utterly dependent on the work of the Holy Spirit for regeneration.

God's Power in Your Life

The Indwelling Spirit

When one is born of the Spirit, the Spirit takes up His abode in him. (See 1 Corinthians 3:16; 6:19.) The Holy Spirit dwells in everyone who belongs to Christ (Romans 8:9). We may not have surrendered our lives utterly to this indwelling Spirit, we may be very far from being full of the Spirit, and we may be very imperfect Christians. But if we have been born again, the Spirit dwells in us, just as He did in the Corinthians, who were certainly far from being perfect Christians.

> **We must feed on the Word of God.**

What a glorious thought it is that the Holy Spirit dwells in me! But it is also a very solemn thought as well. If my body is the temple of the Holy Spirit (1 Corinthians 6:19), I certainly should not defile it, as many professed Christians do. Bearing in mind that our bodies are temples of the Holy Spirit would solve many problems that perplex young Christians.

The Spirit Gives Satisfaction

We find a further thought about the power of the Holy Spirit in John 4:14: *"But whosoever drinketh of the water that I shall give him shall never thirst; but the water that I shall give him shall be in him a well of water springing up into everlasting life."* You may not see at first that this verse has anything to do with the Holy Spirit, but compare it with John 7:37–39, and it will be evident that the water here symbolizes the Holy Spirit. So the Holy Spirit then has the power to give abiding and everlasting satisfaction.

Of every worldly joy, it must be said, *"Whosoever drinketh of this water shall thirst again"* (John 4:13). The world can never satisfy. But the Holy Spirit has the power to satisfy every longing of the soul. The Holy Spirit, and He alone, can satisfy the human heart. If you give yourself up to the Holy Spirit's inflowing—or rather upspringing—in your heart, you will never thirst. You will not long for worldly gain or honor.

If we are born again, the Spirit dwells in us.

The Holy Spirit has poured the unutterable joy and indescribable satisfaction of His living water into many souls. Have you felt this living fountain within you? Is it springing up without restraint into everlasting life?

The Spirit Offers Freedom

In Romans 8:2, we read, *"For the law of the Spirit of life in Christ Jesus hath made me free from the law of sin and death."* The Holy Spirit has the power to set us *"free from the law of sin and death."* What *"the law of sin and death"* is can be found in the preceding chapter. (See Romans 7:9–24.)

Read this description carefully. We all know this *"law of sin and death"*; we have all been in bondage to it. Some of us are still in bondage to it, but we do not need to be.

God has provided a way of escape by the Holy Spirit's power. When we give up the hopeless struggle of trying to overcome *"the law of sin and death"* with our own strength and, in utter helplessness, surrender to the Holy Spirit to do everything for us—when we walk in His blessed power rather than in the power of the flesh—then He sets us *"free from the law of sin and death."*

It is our privilege to have victory over sin.

Many professing Christians today live as is described in Romans 7. Some go so far as to maintain that the normal Christian life is a life of constant defeat. This would be true if we were left to ourselves, for in ourselves, we are *"carnal, sold under sin"* (verse 14). But we are not left to ourselves. The Holy Spirit undertakes for us what we fail to do ourselves (Romans 8:2–4).

The True Christian Life

Romans 8 gives us a picture of the true Christian life. This life is possible, and God expects it from each one of us. The commandment comes to this life (see Romans 7), but the mighty Spirit comes also, working obedience and victory.

The Power of the Holy Spirit

The flesh is still in us, but we are not in the flesh. (See Romans 8:9, 12–13.) We do not live after it. We walk *"after to the Spirit"* (verse 4). *"Through the Spirit* [we] *do mortify the deeds of the body"* (verse 13). We *"walk in the Spirit"* and do *"not fulfil the lust of the flesh"* (Galatians 5:16).

It is our privilege, in the Spirit's power, to have daily, hourly, and constant victory over the flesh and over sin. But the victory is not in ourselves, not in any strength of our own. Left to ourselves, deserted by the Spirit of God, we would be as helpless as ever. It is all in the Spirit's power. If we try to take one step in our own strength, we will fail.

Has the Holy Spirit set you *"free from the law of sin and death"* (Romans 8:2)? Will you let Him do it now? Simply give up all self-effort to stop sinning. Believe in the divine power of the Holy Spirit to set you free, and give yourself to Him to do it. He will not fail you. Then you can triumphantly cry with Paul, *"The law of the Spirit of life in Christ Jesus hath made me free from the law of sin and death"* (verse 2).

The Spirit Strengthens the Believer

We find a closely allied but larger thought about the Holy Spirit's power in Ephesians 3:16: *"That he would grant you, according to the riches of his glory, to be strengthened with might by his Spirit in the inner man."*

God's Power in Your Life

The Holy Spirit strengthens the believer with power in the inner man. The result of this strengthening is seen in Ephesians 3:17–19. Here, the power of the Spirit manifests itself not merely in giving us victory over sin but in Christ's dwelling in our hearts (verse 17); our being *rooted and grounded in love* (verse 17); and our being made *able to comprehend with all saints what is the breadth, and length, and depth, and height; and to know the love of Christ, which passeth knowledge* (verses 18–19). It culminates in our being *filled with all the fulness of God* (verse 19).

The Spirit Guides the Life

We find a further thought about the Holy Spirit's power in Romans 8:14: *For as many as are led by the Spirit of God, they are the sons of God.* The Holy Spirit has the power to lead us into a holy life—a life as *sons of God,* a godlike life. Not only does the Holy Spirit give us the power to live holy lives that are pleasing to God, but He also takes us by the hand and leads us into those lives.

All we must do is simply surrender ourselves completely to His leading and molding. Those who do this are not merely God's offspring (which all men are, according to Acts 17:28), neither are they merely God's children—these are *sons of God.*

Later in the chapter, there is a new thought: *The Spirit itself beareth witness with our spirit, that we are the children of God"* (Romans 8:16). The Holy Spirit bears witness with the spirit of the believer that he is a child of God. Note that Paul did not say that the Spirit bears witness *to* our spirit, but *with* it—*"with our spirit"* is the exact force of the words used.

In other words, there are two who bear witness to our sonship: Our spirits and the Holy Spirit bear witness together that we are children of God. How does the Holy Spirit bear His testimony to this fact? Galatians 4:6 answers this question: *"Because ye are sons, God hath sent forth the Spirit of his Son into your hearts, crying, Abba, Father."* The Holy Spirit Himself enters our hearts and cries, *"Abba, Father."*

> **The Holy Spirit strengthens the believer.**

Note the order of the Spirit's work in Romans 8:2, 4, 13–14, 16. He bears witness in us (verse 16) only when *"the law of the Spirit of life in Christ Jesus hath made [us] free from the law of sin and death"* (verse 2) so that *"the righteousness of the law might be fulfilled in us, who walk not after the flesh, but after the Spirit"* (verse 4). Only when we *"through the Spirit do mortify the deeds of the body"* (verse 13) and when we are surrendered to the Spirit's leading (verse 14) can we expect to experience the promise in verse 16 and have the clear assurance that comes from the Spirit of God testifying together with our spirits *"that we are children of God"* (verse 16).

Many believers expect this witness of the Holy Spirit to precede their surrendering wholly to God and their confessing Jesus Christ as their Savior and Lord, which is incorrect. The testimony of the Holy Spirit to our sonship comes only after all this is done.

The Spirit Gives Christlikeness

An exceedingly important thought about the Holy Spirit's power is found in Galatians 5:22–23: *"But the fruit of the Spirit is love, joy, peace, longsuffering, gentleness, goodness, faith, meekness, temperance: against such there is no law."*

The Holy Spirit brings forth Christlike graces of character in the believer. (See Romans 14:17; 15:13; 5:5.) All real beauty of character—all real Christlikeness in us—is the Holy Spirit's work. It is His *"fruit."* He bears it, not us. Note that these graces are not said to be the *fruits* of the Spirit; they are the *"fruit."* All the various manifestations of the Holy Spirit have the same origin. Therefore, not just some of them, but all, will appear in everyone in whom the Holy Spirit is given full control.

It is a beautiful life that is set forth in these verses. Every word is worthy of earnest study and profound meditation: *love, joy, peace, longsuffering, gentleness, goodness, faith, meekness, temperance.* The Christ-life is the life we long for. It is not natural to us, and it is not attainable by any effort of the flesh. The life that is natural for us is described in the three preceding verses (Galatians 5:19–21).

But when we give the indwelling Spirit full control, realizing the evilness of the flesh and giving up ever attaining anything good in its power—when we come to the end of self—then these holy graces of character become His fruit in us.

If you desire these graces in your character and in your life, renounce yourself and all your attempts at holiness. Then let the Holy Spirit, who dwells in you, take full control and bear His own glorious fruit. Live in the reality expressed (from another point of view) in Galatians 2:20:

Let the Spirit bear His own glorious fruit.

> *I am crucified with Christ: nevertheless I live; yet not I, but Christ liveth in me: and the life which I now live in the flesh I live by the faith of the Son of God, who loved me, and gave himself for me.*

The Flesh Never Bears Christlikeness

Realize from the start that the flesh can never bear the fruit of the Spirit, that you can never attain these things on your own. Those who study ethical philosophy would like us to believe that the flesh can be cultivated until it bears this fruit. But it cannot be done until thorns can be made to bear figs, and a bramble bush bear grapes. (See Luke 6:44; Matthew 12:33.)

Others talk about character-building. Nothing is essentially wrong with this, but if you let the Holy Spirit do the building, it becomes not so much building as fruit-bearing. There is also a good deal said about cultivating graces of character. But we must always bear in mind that the way to cultivate the true graces of character is by submitting ourselves entirely to the Spirit. This is *"sanctification of the Spirit"* (1 Peter 1:2).

We have a divine teacher: the Holy Spirit.

We turn now to another aspect of the power of the Holy Spirit.

The Spirit Guides into Truth

Howbeit when he, the Spirit of truth, is come, he will guide you into all truth: for he shall not speak of himself; but whatsoever he shall hear, that shall he speak: and he will show you things to come. (John 16:13)

The Holy Spirit has the power to guide the believer *"into all truth."* This promise was originally made to the apostles, but the apostles themselves applied it to all believers (1 John 2:20, 27).

The Power of the Holy Spirit

It is the privilege of each of us to be *"taught of God"* (John 6:45). Each believer is independent of human teachers. *"Ye need not that any man teach you"* (1 John 2:27). This does not mean, of course, that we may not learn much from others who are themselves taught by the Holy Spirit. If John had thought that, he never would have written this epistle to teach others.

The man who can be most fully taught by God is the one who is most ready to listen to what God has taught others. This does not mean that when we are taught by God we are independent of the Word of God. The Word is the very place to which the Spirit leads His pupils and the instrument through which He teaches them. (See John 6:63; Ephesians 5:18–19; 6:17; Colossians 3:16.)

But we should not be dependent on men, even though we can learn much from them. We have a divine teacher: the Holy Spirit. We will never truly know the truth until we are taught by Him. No amount of mere human teaching, no matter who our teachers may be, will give us a correct understanding of the truth. Not even a diligent study of the Word, either in English or in the original languages, will give us a real understanding of the truth. We must be taught by the Holy Spirit.

The one who is thus taught, even if he does not know a word of Greek or Hebrew, will understand the truth of God better than someone who does know the original languages but who is not taught by the Spirit. The Spirit will guide the one He teaches *"into all truth"* (John 16:13)—not in a day, a week, or a year, but one step at a time.

There are two especially important aspects of the Spirit's teaching: *"He will show you things to come"* (verse 13). Many say we can know nothing about the future, that all our thoughts on that subject are nothing but guesswork. Anyone taught by the Spirit knows better than that.

The Spirit reveals and glorifies Christ.

Second, *"He shall glorify me: for he shall receive of mine, and shall show it unto you"* (John 16:14). The Holy Spirit's special area of instruction, with the believer as well as the unbeliever, is to reveal Christ and glorify Him. Many fear to emphasize this truth about the Holy Spirit because it might overshadow Christ. Actually, though, no one magnifies Christ as the Holy Spirit does.

We will never understand Christ, nor see His glory, until the Holy Spirit reveals Him to us. Merely listening to sermons and lectures, even studying the Word, will never present Christ as He can. And He is longing to do so. Let the Holy Spirit do His glorious work in you. Christ is so different when the Holy Spirit magnifies Him by taking the things of Christ and showing them to us (John 16:15).

The Power of the Holy Spirit

The Spirit Teaches Christ's Words

Turning to John 14:26, we again find the Holy Spirit's power to teach, but with an added thought: *"But the Comforter, which is the Holy Ghost, whom the Father will send in my name, he shall teach you all things, and bring all things to your remembrance, whatsoever I have said unto you."* The Holy Spirit has the power to bring to our remembrance the words of Christ.

This promise was made primarily to the apostles, and it guarantees the accuracy of their report of what Jesus said. But the Holy Spirit works similarly in each believer who expects it of Him and looks to Him to do it.

He brings to mind the teachings and the words of Christ, just when we need them, for either the necessities of our own life or our Christian service. How often have we been distressed about something or lost as to what to say to someone we wanted to help. Just then, the Scripture we needed—probably some passage we had not thought of for a long time, perhaps never thought of in this connection—was brought to mind. It was the Holy Spirit who did this, and He is ready to do it even more when we expect it of Him.

It is not without significance that in the next verse, after making this great promise, Jesus said, *"Peace I leave with you, My peace I give to you"* (John 14:27). Look to the Holy Spirit to bring the right words to remembrance at the right time, and you will have peace. This is the way to remember Scripture just when you need it and just the Scripture you need.

The Spirit Reveals Mysteries

Closely related to what has been said in the two preceding sections is the power of the Holy Spirit as seen in 1 Corinthians 2:10–14:

> *But God hath revealed them unto us by his Spirit: for the Spirit searcheth all things, yea, the deep things of God. For what man knoweth the things of a man, save the spirit of man which is in him? even so the things of God knoweth no man, but the Spirit of God. Now we have received, not the spirit of the world, but the spirit which is of God; that we might know the things that are freely given to us of God. Which things also we speak, not in the words which man's wisdom teacheth, but which the Holy Ghost teacheth; comparing spiritual things with spiritual. But the natural man receiveth not the things of the Spirit of God: for they are foolishness unto him: neither can he know them, because they are spiritually discerned.*

The Spirit interprets His own revelation.

In these verses, we see a twofold work of the Spirit: First, the Holy Spirit reveals to us the deep things of God that are hidden from, and foolishness to, the natural man. It is preeminently to the apostles the Spirit did this, but His work is not limited to them. Second, the Holy Spirit interprets His own revelation, or imparts power to discern, know, and appreciate what He has taught.

Not only is the Holy Spirit the Author of revelation—the written Word of God—He is also the Interpreter of what He has revealed. How much more interesting and useful any profound book becomes when we have the author of the book right at hand to interpret it for us!

This is what we may always have when we study the Bible. The Author—the Holy Spirit— is right at hand to interpret. To understand the Bible, we must look to Him. Then, even the darkest places become clear. We need to pray often with the psalmist, *"Open thou mine eyes, that I may behold wondrous things out of thy law"* (Psalm 119:18).

It is not enough for us to have the objective revelation of the written Word. We must also have the inward illumination of the Holy Spirit to enable us to comprehend it. Trying to comprehend a spiritual revelation with natural understanding is a great mistake.

Consider a man who has no sense of aesthetics expecting to appreciate a fine painting simply because he is not color-blind. It would be the same for a man who was not filled with the Spirit to try to understand the Bible simply because he understood the grammar and the vocabulary of the language in which the Bible was written.

I would no more think of allowing a man to teach art merely because he understood paints than of allowing him to teach the Bible merely because he understood Greek or Hebrew.

Utter Insufficiency

Not only must we recognize the utter insufficiency and worthlessness of our own righteousness (the lesson of the opening chapters of Romans), but also the utter insufficiency and worthlessness of our own wisdom in comprehending the things of God (the lesson of the first epistle to the Corinthians).

The Jews had a revelation from the Spirit, but they failed to depend on Him to interpret it for them, so they went astray. The whole evangelical church realizes the utter insufficiency of man's righteousness, theoretically at least. Now it needs to be taught, and made to feel, the utter insufficiency of man's wisdom. That is perhaps the lesson this century of arrogant, intellectual conceit needs more than any other. To understand God's Word, we must totally disregard our own wisdom and rest in utter dependence on the Spirit of God to interpret it for us. (See Matthew 11:25.)

Only when we put away our own righteousness will we find the righteousness of God. (See Philippians 3:4–9; Romans 10:3.) Only when we put away our own wisdom will we find the wisdom of God. (See 1 Corinthians 3:18; Matthew 11:25; 1 Corinthians 1:25–28.) And only when we put away our own strength will we find the strength of God. (See Isaiah 40:29; 2 Corinthians 12:9; 1 Corinthians 1:27–28.)

> **Emptying must always precede filling.**

Emptying must precede filling. Self must be poured out so that Christ may be poured in. We must be taught daily by the Holy Spirit to understand the Word of God. I cannot depend today on the fact that the Spirit taught me yesterday. Each new contact with the Word must be in the power of the Spirit. That the Holy Spirit once illumined our minds to grasp a certain passage is not enough. He must do so each time we confront that passage.

Andrew Murray, in his book *The Spirit of Christ*,* states this truth well. He said, "Each time you come to the Word in study, in hearing a sermon or reading a religious book, there should be a

---

* Available from Whitaker House.

definite act of self-relinquishment, denying your own wisdom and yielding yourself in faith to the Divine Teacher."

The Spirit Helps Us Communicate

The Holy Spirit not only has the power to teach us the truth, but He also helps us communicate that truth to others. We see this brought out again and again:

And I, brethren, when I came to you, came not with excellency of speech or of wisdom, declaring unto you the testimony of God. For I determined not to know any thing among you, save Jesus Christ, and him crucified. And I was with you in weakness, and in fear, and in much trembling. And my speech and my preaching was not with enticing words of man's wisdom, but in demonstration of the Spirit and of power: that your faith should not stand in the wisdom of men, but in the power of God. (1 Corinthians 2:1–5)

The Spirit helps us to communicate powerfully.

Our gospel came not unto you in word only, but also in power, and in the Holy Ghost.
(1 Thessalonians 1:5)

But ye shall receive power, after that the Holy Ghost is come upon you. (Acts 1:8)

The Holy Spirit enables the believer to communicate powerfully to others the truth he himself has been taught. We not only need the

Holy Spirit to reveal and then to interpret the truth He has revealed, but we also need Him to enable us to effectively communicate that truth to others. We need Him every step of the way.

One great cause of real failure in the ministry, even when there is apparent success (not only in the ministry, but in all forms of Christian service), is the attempt to teach what the Holy Spirit has taught us by *"enticing words of man's wisdom"* (1 Corinthians 2:4), human logic, rhetoric, or eloquence. What is needed is Holy Spirit power, a *"demonstration of the Spirit and of power"* (verse 4).

Causes of Failure

There are three causes of failure in Christian work. First, a message other than the message that the Holy Spirit has revealed in the Word is taught. Men will preach science, art, philosophy, sociology, history, experience, etc., but not the Word of God as found in the Holy Spirit's Book—the Bible. Second, the Spirit's message, the Bible, is studied without the Spirit's illumination. Third, the Bible is taught to others with *"enticing words of man's wisdom,"* and not *"in demonstration of the Spirit and of power"* (verse 4).

We must be absolutely dependent on the Holy Spirit when it comes to God's Word. He must teach us how to speak as well as what to speak. His must be the power as well as the message.

75

The Spirit Teaches Prayer

The Holy Spirit has the power to teach us how to pray. In Jude 20, we read, *"But ye, beloved, building up yourselves on your most holy faith, praying in the Holy Ghost."* And again in Ephesians 6:18, *"Praying always...in the Spirit."*

The Holy Spirit guides the believer in prayer. The disciples did not know how to pray as they should, so they came to Jesus and said, *"Lord, teach us to pray"* (Luke 11:1). *"We know not what we should pray for as we ought"* (Romans 8:26), but we have another Helper right at hand to help us (John 14:16–17). *"The Spirit also helpeth our infirmities"* (Romans 8:26).

> **True prayer is prayer in the Spirit.**

He teaches us to pray. True prayer is prayer *"in the Spirit"* (Ephesians 6:18), the prayer that the Spirit inspires and directs. When we come into God's presence to pray, we should recognize our ignorance of what we should pray for or how we should pray. With this awareness, we should then look to the Holy Spirit and cast ourselves utterly on Him to direct our prayers.

Pray in the Spirit

Rushing heedlessly into God's presence and asking the first thing that comes to our minds, or what someone asks us to pray for, is not praying *"in the Spirit"* and is not true prayer. We must wait for and surrender ourselves to the Holy Spirit. The prayer that the Holy Spirit inspires is the prayer that God the Father answers.

From Romans 8:26–27, we learn that the longings that the Holy Spirit creates in our hearts are often too deep for utterance; too deep, apparently, for clear and definite comprehension on the part of the believer himself, in whom the Holy Spirit is working. God Himself must search the heart to know *"what is the mind of the Spirit"* (verse 27) in these unuttered and unutterable longings. But God does know *"what is the mind of the Spirit."* He does know what those Spirit-given longings mean, even if we do not.

These longings are *"according to his purpose"* (verse 28), and He grants them. He is *"able to do exceeding abundantly above all that we ask or think, according to the power that worketh in us"* (Ephesians 3:20). Other times, the Spirit's leadings in prayer are so plain that we *"pray with the spirit, and...with the understanding"* (1 Corinthians 14:15).

The Spirit Offers Thanks

The Holy Spirit also has the power to lead our hearts in acceptable thanksgiving to God. Paul said:

Be filled with the Spirit; speaking to yourselves in psalms and hymns and spiritual songs, singing and

making melody in your heart to the Lord; giving thanks always for all things unto God and the Father in the name of our Lord Jesus Christ.
(Ephesians 5:18–20)

Not only does the Spirit teach us to pray, but He also teaches us to give thanks. One of the most prominent characteristics of the Spirit-filled life is thanksgiving. True thanksgiving is *"unto God and the Father in the name of our Lord Jesus Christ"* (verse 20) and in the Holy Spirit.

The Spirit Inspires Worship

The Holy Spirit has the power to inspire worship that is acceptable to God in the heart of the believer. *"For we are the circumcision, which worship God in the spirit, and rejoice in Christ Jesus, and have no confidence in the flesh"* (Philippians 3:3). Prayer is not worship; thanksgiving is not worship. Worship is a definite act of the believer in relation to God. Worship is bowing before God in adoring acknowledgment and contemplation of Him.

Someone has said, "In our prayers we are taken up with our needs, in our thanksgivings we are taken up with our blessings, and in our worship we are taken up with Himself." There is no true and acceptable worship except what the Holy Spirit inspires and guides. *"For the Father seeketh such to worship him"* (John 4:23).

The flesh seeks to enter every sphere of life. It has its worship as well as its lust. The worship that the flesh prompts is an abomination to God. Not all earnest and honest worship is worship *"in the Spirit"* (Philippians 3:3). A person's worship may be very honest and earnest; still, it

The Spirit inspires acceptable worship.

may not be led by the Holy Spirit, so it remains in the flesh. Even where there is great loyalty to the letter of the Word, worship may not be *"in the Spirit."*

To worship properly, we must *"have no confidence in the flesh"* (Philippians 3:3). We must recognize the utter inability of the flesh (the natural self, as contrasted with the divine Spirit who dwells in and molds the believer) to worship acceptably. We must also realize the danger of the flesh—self—intruding into our worship. In complete self-distrust and self-denial, we must ask the Holy Spirit to lead us to worship correctly. Just as we must renounce our self-worth and look to the crucified Christ for justification, we must renounce our self-righteousness and give ourselves completely to the Holy Spirit for His guidance in praying, giving thanks, worshipping, living, and in everything else that we do.

The Spirit Calls to the Ministry

Let us consider the Holy Spirit's power as a guide. In Acts 13:2–4, we read,

> *As they ministered to the Lord, and fasted, the Holy Ghost said, Separate me Barnabas and Saul for the work whereunto I have called them. And when they had fasted and prayed, and laid their hands on them, they sent them away. So they, being sent forth by the Holy Ghost, departed unto Seleucia; and from thence they sailed to Cyprus.*

People are called and sent forth by the Holy Spirit to particular types of work. He not only calls in a general way into Christian work but also selects the specific work and points it out. "Should I go to China, to Africa, or to India?" a believer might ask. You cannot answer that question for yourself, and no one else can answer it for you. Besides, not every Christian is called to China or Africa or any other foreign field. God alone knows whether He wishes you to go to any of these places, and He is willing to show you.

How does the Holy Spirit call? The passage before us does not say. It is, presumably, intentionally silent on this point to prevent our thinking that He must always call in precisely the same way. Nothing indicates that He spoke in an audible voice, much less that He made His will known in any of the fantastic ways in which some profess to discern His leading (as by opening the Bible at random). But the important point is that He made His will clearly known.

He is as willing to make His will clearly known to us today. The great need in present-day Christian work is men and women whom the Holy Spirit calls and sends forth. We have plenty of people whom **He is willing** *men* have called and sent forth, **to make His** and we have far too many *who* **will clearly** *have called themselves.* How do we **known.** receive the Holy Spirit's call? By desiring it, seeking it, waiting on the Lord for it, and expecting it. *"As they ministered to the Lord, and fasted"* (Acts 13:2), the record reads.

Many Christians say they have never been called by the Spirit. How do they know that? Have they been listening for it? God often speaks in a still, small voice, which only the attentive ear can perceive. Have you definitely offered yourself to God to be used by Him? While no one should go to China or Africa unless he is clearly called, he should definitely offer himself to God to be used *somehow* by Him. He should then be ready for a call and listen carefully so that he hears it when it comes.

The Spirit Guides Us

In these verses, we learn something further about the Holy Spirit's power to guide us.

And he arose and went: and, behold, a man of Ethiopia, an eunuch of great authority under Candace queen of the Ethiopians, who had the charge of all her treasure, and had come to Jerusalem for to worship, was returning, and sitting in his chariot read Esaias the prophet. Then the Spirit said unto Philip, Go near, and join thyself to this chariot. (Acts 8:27–29)

We can have the Spirit's unerring guidance.

And in Acts 16:6–7, we read,

Now when they had gone throughout Phrygia and the region of Galatia, and were forbidden of the Holy Ghost to preach the word in Asia, after they were come to Mysia, they assayed to go into Bithynia: but the Spirit suffered them not.

The Holy Spirit guides us in our daily lives and service, showing us where to go and where not to go, what to do and what not to do. It is possible for us to have the unerring guidance of the Holy Spirit at every turn in our lives.

For example, God does not expect an evangelist to speak to every person he meets. There are some to whom we should not speak. Time spent on them could be time taken from work that would be more to the glory of God. Doubtless, Philip met many people as he journeyed toward Gaza before he met the one of whom the Spirit said, *"Go near, and join thyself to this chariot"* (Acts 8:29).

In the same way, the Holy Spirit is ready to guide us in our personal work. He is also ready to guide us in all of our affairs—business, school, social life, everything. We can have God's wisdom if we desire it. There is no promise more simple and explicit than James 1:5: *"If any of you lack wisdom, let him ask of God, that giveth to all men liberally, and upbraideth not; and it shall be given him."*

The Way to Wisdom

How do we gain this wisdom? James 1:5–7 answers this question. There are really five steps:

(1) We must be conscious of and fully admit our own inability to decide wisely. Not only the sinfulness, but the wisdom of the flesh, must be renounced.

(2) We must sincerely desire to know God's way and be willing to do God's will. This is a point of fundamental importance. Here we find the reason why many believers do not

know God's will and do not have the Spirit's guidance. They are simply not willing to do whatever the Spirit leads them to do. It is the *"meek will he guide in judgment: and the meek will he teach his way"* (Psalm 25:9). The Christian who *"will do His will"* is the Christian who *"shall know"* (John 7:17).

(3) We must definitely *ask* for guidance.

(4) We must confidently *expect* guidance. *"Let him ask in faith, nothing wavering"* (James 1:6).

(5) We must follow, step by step, as the guidance comes. Just how it will come no one can tell, but it will come. It may come with only one step made clear at a time. But that is all we really need to know. Too many believers remain in darkness because they do not know what God wants them to do next week, next month, or next year. To know just the next step is enough. Take it, and then He will show you the next. (See Numbers 9:17–23.)

God's Way Is Made Clear

God's guidance is clear guidance (John 1:5). You may, at some point, believe the Spirit is leading you to do a particular thing, but you are not certain. As God's child, you have a right to be sure. Go to Him and say, "Heavenly Father, please let me know if this is Your will, and I will gladly do it." He will answer you, and you should do nothing until He does.

However, we have no right to dictate to God how He should give His guidance to us. Although we may ask for and expect wisdom, we may not dictate how it is to be given. (See 1 Corinthians 12:11.)

The Spirit Gives Boldness

There is one more dimension to the Holy Spirit's power. Read Acts 4:31: *"And when they had prayed, the place was shaken where they were assembled together; and they were all filled with the Holy Ghost, and they spake the word of God with boldness."* The Holy Spirit has the power to give us boldness in our testimony for Christ.

God's guidance is clear guidance.

Many people are naturally shy. They long to do something for Christ, but they are afraid. The Holy Spirit can make you bold if you will look to Him and trust Him to do it. It was He who turned the cowardly Peter into the one who fearlessly faced the Sanhedrin and rebuked their sin. (See Acts 4:8–12.)

The Power of the Spirit

Two things stand out in what has been said about the power of the Holy Spirit in the believer. First, we are utterly dependent on Him in every aspect of Christian life and service. Second, because of the Holy Spirit's work, God's provision for that life and service is a fullness of privilege that is open to even the humblest believer.

It is not of much importance what we are by nature—either intellectually, morally, spiritually, or even physically. What **The Holy** matters is what the Holy Spirit **Spirit can** can do for us and what we will **make us** let Him do. The Holy Spirit **bold.** often takes the one who seems the least promising and uses him far more than those who seem the most promising.

Christian life is not to be lived in the realm of natural temperament but in the realm of the Spirit. And Christian work is not to be done in the power of natural endowment but in the power of the Spirit. The Holy Spirit eagerly desires to do His whole work for each of us. He will do for us everything we will let Him do.

Chapter 4
The Power
of Prayer

four

The Power of Prayer

Power belongeth unto God" (Psalm 62:11), but all that belongs to God, we can have for the asking. God holds out His full hands and says,

> Ask, and it shall be given you....If ye then, being evil, know how to give good gifts unto your children, how much more shall your Father which is in heaven give good things to them that ask him?   (Matthew 7:7, 11)

The poverty and powerlessness of the average Christian find their explanation in the words of the apostle James: "Yet ye have not, because ye ask not" (James 4:2).

Because You Do Not Ask

"Why is it," a Christian may ask, "that I make such poor progress in my Christian life?"

"Neglect of prayer," God answers. "You do not have because you do not ask."

"Why is it there is so little fruit in my ministry?" asks many a discouraged minister.

"Neglect of prayer," God answers again. "You do not have because you do not ask."

"Why is it," both ministers and laymen are asking, "that there is so little power in my life and service?"

And again God answers, "Neglect of prayer. 'You do not have because you do not ask.'"

God has provided a life of power for every child of His. He has put His own infinite power at our disposal and has proclaimed over and over in a great variety of ways in His Word, *"Ask, and it shall be given you"* (Matthew 7:7; Luke 11:9). Thousands upon thousands have taken God at His word in this matter, and they have always found it true.

Power

The first Christians were men and women of tremendous power. For example, what power Peter and John had in their lives! What power they had in their work! There was opposition in those days—most determined, bitter, and relentless opposition, that, in comparison, would make any that we might encounter appear like child's play—but the work went right on.

We constantly read such statements as these:

> *The Lord added to the church daily such as should be saved.* (Acts 2:47)

> *Howbeit many of them which heard the word believed; and the number of the men was about five thousand.* (Acts 4:4)

> *And believers were the more added to the Lord, multitudes both of men and women.* (Acts 5:14)

The apostles themselves explained the secret of their irresistible power when they said, *"We will give ourselves continually to prayer, and to the ministry of the word"* (Acts 6:4). But it was not only the leaders of that early church who had power in life and service; so did the rank and file. What a beautiful picture we have of their abounding love and fruit-fulness! (See Acts 2:44–47; 4:32–37; 8:4; 11:19, 21.) The secret of this fullness of power in life and service is found in Acts 2:42: *"They continued stedfastly...in prayers."*

God delights in answering our prayers.

In the Lord's Presence

God delights to answer prayer. *"Call upon me in the day of trouble,"* He cries. *"I will deliver thee, and thou shalt glorify me"* (Psalm 50:15). There is a place where strength can always be renewed; that place is the presence of the Lord. *"They that wait upon the* LORD *shall renew their strength; they shall mount up with wings as eagles; they shall run, and not be weary; and they shall walk, and not faint"* (Isaiah 40:31).

How little time the average Christian spends in prayer! We are too busy to pray, and so we are too busy to have power. We have a great deal of activity, but we accomplish little; there are many services, but few conversions. The power of God is lacking in our lives and in our work. We do not have because we do not ask (James 4:2).

Many Christians confess that they do not believe in the power of prayer. Some go so far as to contemptuously contrast the pray-ers with the doers—forgetting that in the history of the church, the real doers have been pray-ers. Without exception, those who have made the church's history glorious have been people of prayer.

A Mighty Weapon

Of those who do believe theoretically in the power of prayer, not one in a thousand realizes its power. How much time does the average Christian spend daily in prayer? How much time do you spend daily in prayer?

It was a masterstroke of the Devil to get the church and the ministry to lay aside the mighty weapon of prayer. He does not mind at all if the church expands her organizations and her deftly contrived machinery for the conquest of the world for Christ if she will only give up praying. He laughs softly as he looks at the church of today and says under his breath, "You can have your Sunday schools, your social organizations, your grand choirs, and even your revival efforts, as long as you do not bring the power of almighty God into them by earnest, persistent, and believing prayer."

We do not have because we do not ask.

The Devil is not afraid of organizations; he is only afraid of God. And organizations without prayer are organizations without God.

Our day is characterized by the increase of man's machinery and the decrease of God's power sought and obtained by prayer. But when men and women arise who believe in prayer and who pray in the way the Bible teaches us to pray, prayer accomplishes as much as it ever did. Today's prayer can do as much as the early church's prayer. All the infinite resources of God are at its command.

The Key to God's Grace

Prayer can do anything God can do, for the arm of God responds to its touch. Prayer is the key that opens the inexhaustible storehouses of divine grace and power. *"Ask, and it shall be given you*" (Matthew 7:7), cries our heavenly Father, as He swings the doors of His treasure-house open wide. The only limit to what prayer can do is what God can do. But all things are possible with God (Matthew 19:26); therefore, prayer is omnipotent.

Christian history and Christian biography demonstrate the truth of what the Word of God teaches about prayer. All through the history of the church, men and women have arisen in all ranks of life who believed with simple, child-like faith what the Bible teaches about prayer. They have asked, and they have received. But what are some of the definite things that prayer has the power to do?

Prayer opens the storehouse of God's grace.

Prayer Brings Knowledge

Prayer has the power to bring us a true knowledge of ourselves and our needs. Nothing is more necessary than for us to know ourselves: our weaknesses, our sinfulness, our selfishness; how in us (that is to say, in our flesh) "*dwelleth no good thing*" (Romans 7:18). Lives of power have usually begun with a revelation of the utter powerlessness and worthlessness of self.

So it was with Isaiah. In the year that King Uzziah died, he was brought face-to-face with God, saw himself, and cried out, "*Woe is me! for*

I am undone; because I am a man of unclean lips" (Isaiah 6:5). Then a life of power began for Isaiah as God sent him forth to a mighty work. (See Isaiah 6:8–9.)

So it was with Moses. He met God at the burning bush, where he was emptied of his former self-confidence and saw his utter unfitness for the Lord's work. Then the Lord sent him to Pharaoh as a mighty man of power. (See Exodus 3:2, 5, 11; compare with his former self-confidence in Exodus 2:12–15.)

Prayer has the power to bring true knowledge.

And so it was with Job. It was after Job met God and cried, concerning himself, *"I abhor myself, and repent in dust and ashes"* (Job 42:6), that the Lord released him from captivity, giving him power to intercede for his friends and to bear abundant fruit.

If we are to have fullness of power, it is necessary that we see ourselves as we are by nature in the flesh. This is accomplished through prayer. If we sincerely pray the psalmist's prayer, *"Search me, O God, and know my heart: try me, and know my thoughts"* (Psalm 139:23), He will do it.

But to pray this prayer just once is not enough; it needs to be repeated daily. Then we will come to see ourselves as God sees us. There will be a consequent emptying of self, making room for the incoming of the power of God.

Prayer Cleanses from Sin

Prayer has the power to cleanse our hearts from sin—from secret sins and from known sins (Psalm 19:12–13). In answer to David's prayer after his disastrous fall, God washed him thoroughly from his iniquity and cleansed him from his sin (Psalm 51:2).

Many have fought for days, months, and years against sins that have been marring their lives and sapping their spiritual power. David finally went to God in prayer, persisting in that prayer until God blessed him, and he emerged a victor from the place of prayer.

In this way, sins that seem unconquerable have been laid in the dust. In this way, sins unknown to the sinner, which have robbed him of power, have been discovered in all their real hideousness and rooted out. Of course, as seen in the previous chapter, it is the Holy Spirit who sets us free from sin's power, but the Holy Spirit works in our lives in answer to our prayers (Luke 11:13).

Prayer has the power to govern our tongues.

Prayer Gives the Victory

Prayer has the power to hold us up in our goings and give us victory over temptation.

The Power of Prayer

"Hold up my goings in thy paths, that my footsteps slip not" (Psalm 17:5), cried David. That is a prayer God is always ready to hear.

In His last hours, Jesus Himself said to His disciples, *"Pray that ye enter not into temptation"* (Luke 22:40). But the disciples did not heed the warning. They slept when they should have prayed, and when the temptation came in a few hours, they failed utterly. But Jesus Himself spent that night in prayer. The next day, when the fiercest temptation that ever attacked a man swept down on Him, He gloriously triumphed.

We can be victorious over every temptation if we will prepare for it and meet it with prayer. Many of us are led into defeat and denial of our Lord, as Peter was, by sleeping when we should have been praying.

Prayer Governs the Tongue

Prayer has the power to govern our tongues. Many Christians who have desired fullness of power in Christian life and service have found themselves kept from it by unruly tongues. They have learned by bitter experiences the truth of the words of James: *"The tongue can no man tame"* (James 3:8). But while no man can tame it, God can and will, in answer to believing prayer.

If one will earnestly pray in faith with David, *"Set a watch, O LORD, before my mouth; keep the door of my lips"* (Psalm 141:3), God will do it. Many unruly tongues have been brought into subjection through this prayer.

Tongues that were as sharp as a sword have learned to speak words of gentleness and grace. True prayer can tame the unruliest tongue by which man or woman was ever cursed because true prayer brings into play the power of Him with whom nothing is impossible (Luke 1:37).

Prayer Brings Wisdom

Prayer has the power to bring us wisdom. The Word of God is very explicit on this point: *"If any of you lack wisdom, let him ask of God, that giveth to all men liberally, and upbraideth not; and it shall be given him"* (James 1:5). No promise could be more explicit than that. We can have wisdom, the wisdom of God Himself, whenever we ask for it.

God does not intend for His children to grope in darkness. He puts His own infinite wisdom at our disposal. All He desires is that we ask, and *"ask in faith"* (verse 6). Many of us are stumbling in our own foolishness, instead of walking in His wisdom, simply because we do not ask.

We can all have the joy of knowing and walking in God's way. It is His great desire to make it known to us. All we have to do is ask. (See Psalm 25:4; 86:11; 119:33; 143:10.)

The Power of Prayer

Prayer Reveals the Word

Prayer has the power to open our eyes to behold wondrous things out of God's Word (Psalm 119:18). It is wonderful how the Bible opens up to someone who looks to God in earnest, believing prayer to interpret it for him. Difficulties vanish; obscure passages become clear as day; and old, familiar portions become luminous with new meaning, living with new power.

Prayer will do more than a theological education to make the Bible an open book. Only people of prayer can understand the Bible.

Prayer Brings the Spirit

Prayer has the power to bring the Holy Spirit in all His blessed power and manifold works into our hearts and lives. Jesus said, *"If ye then, being evil, know how to give good gifts unto your children: how much more shall your heavenly Father give the Holy Spirit to them that ask him?"* (Luke 11:13).

> **God puts His infinite wisdom at our disposal.**

It was after the first disciples had *"continued with one accord in prayer and supplication"* (Acts 1:14) that *"they were all filled with the Holy Ghost"* (Acts 2:4). On another occasion, *"When they had prayed, the place was shaken where they were assembled together; and they were all filled with the Holy Ghost"* (Acts 4:31).

When Peter and John came down to Samaria and found a company of young converts who had not yet experienced the fullness of the Holy Spirit's power, they *"prayed for them, that they might receive the Holy Ghost....Then laid they their hands on them, and they received the Holy Ghost"* (Acts 8:15, 17).

It was in answer to prayer that Paul expected the saints in Ephesus *"to be strengthened with might by his Spirit in the inner man"* (Ephesians 3:16), and that *"the God of our Lord Jesus Christ, the Father of glory,"* would give them *"the spirit of wisdom and revelation in the knowledge of him"* (Ephesians 1:17).

Prayer brings the fullness of the Spirit's power into our hearts and lives. One great reason why so many of us have so little of the Holy Spirit's power in our lives and service is that we spend so little time and thought in prayer. We *"have not, because* [we] *ask not"* (James 4:2).

Every precious, spiritual blessing in our own lives is given by our heavenly Father in answer to true prayer. Prayer promotes our spiritual growth and our likeness to Christ as almost nothing else can. The more time we spend in real, true prayer, the more we will grow in likeness to our Master.

One of the saintliest, most Christlike men who ever lived was John Welch, the son-in-law of John Knox, the great Scottish reformer. Welch is said to have given one-third of his time to prayer, and he often spent a whole night in prayer. Someone who knew him well, speaking of him after he had gone to be with Christ, said of him, "He was a type of Christ."

Many illustrations could be given of the power of prayer to bring our lives into conformity with Christ. In prayer, we gaze into the face of God and *"beholding as in a glass the glory of the Lord, are changed into the same image from glory to glory"* (2 Corinthians 3:18).

The Fullness of Power

But prayer has more to offer than the power to mold us spiritually into the likeness of Christ. It also has the power to bring the fullness of God's power into our work. When the apostolic church saw themselves confronted by obstacles that they could not surmount, *"they lifted up their voice to God with one accord"* (Acts 4:24). *"And when they had prayed"* (verse 31), the power came that swept away all obstacles.

> In prayer, we gaze into the face of God.

Do you desire the power of God in your personal work, in your preaching, or in the training of your children? Pray for it. Hold on to God until you get it. *"Men ought always to pray, and not to faint"* (Luke 18:1).

I will never forget a sight I once witnessed. A woman of limited experience in public speaking was called on to address an audience filling the old Tremont Temple in Boston. It was a notable audience in its makeup as well as in its number. Many leading clergymen of all evangelical denominations were there, as well as men prominent in philanthropic and political affairs.

As the woman spoke, the audience was hushed, swayed, melted, and molded. Tears coursed down cheeks that were unaccustomed to them. The impression made on many was not only good, but permanent. It was an address of marvelous power. The secret of her success lay in the fact, known only to a few, that the woman had spent the whole of the previous night on her face before God in prayer.

We can have all power if we will only believe.

Another example of the power of prayer happened in the 1630s. John Livingstone, a Scottish minister, is said to have spent a full night with several fellow Christians in prayer and discussion of spiritual matters. The next day, he preached in the kirk (church) of Shotts with such power that five hundred souls were saved.

Once, a mother came to me in great distress about her boy, one of the most incorrigible children I ever knew.

The Power of Prayer

"What should I do?" she cried.

"Pray," I answered.

She did so, with new determination, sincerity, and faith. The change came soon, if not immediately, and the change continues to this day.

We can all have power in our work, if we will only believe God's promise regarding prayer. Go to Him often, with a holy boldness that knows He desires to answer you.

Prayer Brings Salvation

The man of prayer can have power in his own life and service as well as power in the life and service of others. Prayer has the power to bring salvation to others. *"If any man see his brother sin a sin which is not unto death, he shall ask, and he shall give him life for them that sin not unto death. There is a sin unto death"* (1 John 5:16). Prayer succeeds in attaining the salvation of others where every other effort fails.

There is little doubt that Saul of Tarsus, the most dangerous human enemy the church ever had, became Paul the apostle in answer to prayer. There have been countless instances where men and women, seemingly beyond all hope, have been converted in quite direct and unmistakable answer to prayer.

The Call for Revival

Prayer will bring blessing on a church. It will settle church quarrels, allay misunderstandings, root out heresy, and bring revivals down from God. Dr. Spencer, in his *Pastor's Sketches,* tells how a great revival was brought to his church by the prayers of a godly old man who was confined to his room due to lameness.

In Philadelphia during the pastorate of Dr. Thomas Skinner, three men of God came together in his study to pray. They wrestled in prayer. As a result, a powerful revival sprang up in that city.

One of the most notable, widespread, and enduring revivals ever known, according to an account given by Charles Finney, rose from the prayers of a humble woman who had never seen a revival but was led to ask God for one.

One of the church's greatest needs is to persevere in calling on God until He visits her again with a mighty outpouring of His Spirit. In past times, there have been great revivals with very little preaching or human effort, but there has never been a great and true revival without abundant prayer. Many modern so-called revivals are contrivances of man's self-effort. Genuine revivals are brought down by prayer.

The Power of Prayer

Prayer Strengthens Ministers

Prayer will bring wisdom and power to ministers of the gospel. Paul was a tremendous preacher and worker, but he so deeply felt the need of the prayers of God's people that he asked for them from every church to which he wrote, except for one (the backslidden church in Galatia).

Genuine revivals are brought by prayer.

It has been demonstrated again and again that prayer can transform a poor preacher into a good one. If you are not satisfied with your pastor, pray for him. Keep on praying for him, and you will soon have a better minister. If you think your present minister is a good one, you can make him even better with more prayer. Little do many Christians realize how much they can influence the powerful or powerless preaching their pastor gives them by their prayer or neglect of prayer.

The power of prayer reaches across the sea and around the earth. We can contribute to the conversion of the heathen and the evangelization of the world by our prayers. The prayers of believers in America have brought down the power of the Spirit in India and China.

Although more men and more money could certainly be used for mission work, its greatest need is prayer. It is a sad fact that much money given to mission work has been largely wasted simply because there has not been enough prayer behind the giving.

Wait upon the Lord

There is mighty power in prayer. It has much to do with our obtaining fullness of power in Christian life and service. Whoever will not take time for prayer may as well give up all hope of obtaining the fullness of power God has for him. It is *"they that wait upon the LORD"* who will *"renew their strength"* (Isaiah 40:31).

True prayer takes both time and thought.

Waiting on God means something more than spending a few minutes at the beginning and close of each day running through some memorized form of request. *"Wait upon the LORD."* True prayer takes time and thought, but ultimately, it is the great time-saver.

No matter what the time or the place, if we are to know fullness of power, we must be men and women of prayer.

Chapter 5
The Power of a Surrendered Life

five

The Power of a
Surrendered Life

Power *belongeth unto God"* (Psalm 62:11),
but there is one condition on which that
power is given to us. That condition is
absolute surrender to Him. In Romans 6:13, we
read, *"Neither yield ye your members as instruments
of unrighteousness unto sin: but yield yourselves unto
God, as those that are alive from the dead, and your
members as instruments of righteousness unto God."*
Again in Romans 6:22, we read, *"But now being
made free from sin, and become servants to God, ye
have your fruit unto holiness, and the end everlasting
life."* The great secret of blessedness and power
is found in these verses.

Surrender to God

"Yield yourselves unto God" (verse 13)—the
whole secret is found in those words. The word

translated *"yield"* means "to put at one's disposal." Put yourselves at God's disposal is the thought. In other words, surrender yourselves absolutely to God, become His property, and allow Him to use you however He wills. This is the wisest thing anyone can do for himself. It secures all the blessedness that is possible to man. Day by day, year by year, God's blessings will be given to him in ever-increasing measure.

If anyone asks, "What is the one thing I can do in order to discover everything that God has for me?" the answer is very simple: Surrender absolutely to God. Say to Him, "Heavenly Father, from now on, I have no will of my own. Let Your will be done in me, through me, by me, and regarding me, in all things. I put myself unreservedly in Your hands. Please do whatever You desire with me."

Absolute surrender is the secret of power.

In response, God, who is infinite love, infinite wisdom, and infinite power, will do His very best with you. You may not immediately see that it is His best, but trust that it is, and sooner or later you will see it. God floods the heart of the believer who surrenders absolutely to Him with light and joy and fills his life with power. Absolute surrender to God is the secret of blessedness and power.

Results of Absolute Surrender

Look at what the Bible says will definitely result from absolute surrender. John 7:17 says, *"If any man will do his will, he shall know of the doctrine."* Knowledge of the truth comes with the surrender of the will. There is nothing like it to clear one's spiritual vision. *"God is light, and in him is no darkness at all"* (1 John 1:5). Surrendering to Him opens our eyes to the light that He Himself is. It brings us at once in harmony with all truth.

Nothing blinds the spiritual vision like self-will or sin. I have seen questions that bothered men for years solved in a very short time when those men simply surrendered to God. What was as dark as night before became as light as day.

The Unsurrendered Will

An unsurrendered will lies behind almost all the skepticism in the world. Are you filled with doubts and questions? Would you like certainty instead of doubt? Yield yourself to God. Would you like to get your feet on the solid rock? Yield yourself to God. Are you trying to feel your way along in the dark? Would you rather see your path clearly before you? Yield yourself to God.

The greatest truths—eternal truths—cannot be learned by mere investigation and study.

They cannot be reasoned out. They must be seen. And the only one who can see them is the one whose eye is cleared by absolute surrender to God. *"If therefore thine eye be single,"* said Jesus, *"thy whole body shall be full of light. But if thine eye be evil, thy whole body shall be full of darkness"* (Matthew 6:22–23). A surrendered life and will is the secret of light and knowledge.

Many people have confided in me that they were wandering in the dark, not knowing what to believe and not quite sure they believed anything. I asked them these questions: "Will you surrender your will to God? Will you give yourself up to God and allow Him to do what He chooses with you?" When their answer was yes, they soon said, "My doubts, my uncertainties, and my darkness are gone. There is nothing but light now."

The Secret of Prevailing Prayer

The next result of a surrendered will and life is power in prayer. The greatest secret of prevailing prayer is what John records from his own joyous experience in 1 John 3:22: *"And whatsoever we ask, we receive of him, because we keep his commandments, and do those things that are pleasing in his sight."* Notice those wonderful words: *"Whatsoever we ask, we receive of him."* Think of it! Not one prayer, great or small, goes unanswered.

The Power of a Surrendered Life

Then notice the reason: *"Because we keep his commandments, and do those things that are pleasing in his sight"* (1 John 3:22). A life entirely surrendered to doing God's will as revealed in His Word and to doing the things that are pleasing in His sight—a life completely at God's disposal—is the secret of prevailing prayer.

Do you wonder why you do not get what you ask for, why you cannot say, like John, "Whatever I ask I get"? It is not because he was an apostle and you are just an ordinary Christian. It is because he could say, "I keep His commandments and do those things (and only those things) that are pleasing in His sight," while you cannot. It is because his life was entirely surrendered to God, while yours is not.

No prayer, great or small, goes unanswered.

Many people are greatly puzzled because their prayers never seem to reach the ears of God but fall back, unanswered, to the earth. There is no mystery about it. It is because they have not met the one great, fundamental condition of prevailing prayer: a surrendered will and a surrendered life. It is when we make God's will ours that He makes our will His. *"Delight thyself also in the LORD; and he shall give thee the desires of thine heart"* (Psalm 37:4).

Jesus said to the Father, *"I knew that thou hearest me always"* (John 11:42). Why did God always hear Him? You say, "Because Jesus was His only begotten Son." But this is not the reason. It was because Jesus could say, *"For I came down from heaven, not to do mine own will, but the will of him that sent me"* (John 6:38); and *"My meat is to do the will of him that sent me"* (John 4:34); and again, *"Lo, I come...to do thy will, O God"* (Hebrews 10:7).

The great secret of prevailing prayer is a surrendered will and a surrendered life. George Müller was preeminent as a powerful man of prayer. Why? Because many years ago, he set out to be and do just what God wanted him to be and do. He pondered God's Word daily and deeply in order to know His will. He yielded himself to God. There is not one of us who cannot become a mighty prince of God if we will do the same thing.

Joy Overflowing

The next result of a surrendered will is a heart overflowing with joy. In the face of the horrible trial and agony through which He was to pass, Jesus said to His disciples,

If ye keep my commandments, ye shall abide in my love; even as I have kept my Father's commandments, and abide in his love. These things

have I spoken unto you, that my joy might remain in you, and that your joy might be full.
(John 15:10–11)

Jesus had found joy in keeping His Father's commandments by completely surrendering to His will. If the disciples would follow that path, His joy would remain in them, and their joy would be *"full."*

The only way to find fullness of joy is through complete, unconditional surrender to God. *"Yield yourselves unto God"* (Romans 6:13). There is no great joy in a half-hearted Christian life. Many Christians have just enough religion to make them miserable. They can no longer enjoy the world, and they have not yet entered *"the joy of the LORD is your strength"* (Nehemiah 8:10). There they stand, deprived of *"the leeks, and the onions, and the garlic"* (Numbers 11:5) of Egypt, yet they are without the milk and honey of Canaan (Exodus 3:8). That is an unhappy place to be. The way out is simple, absolute surrender to God. Then their joy will be fulfilled.

> **There is no joy in a halfhearted Christian life.**

I have known so many who have experienced this fullness of joy. Sometimes it followed a great struggle in which they were afraid to yield absolutely to God, so afraid to say, "O God, I put myself unreservedly into Your hands; do with me what You please." They were afraid God would ask them to do something hard, afraid God might whisper, "China," "India," or "Africa."

Indeed, sometimes He has, and there has been what to the world seemed great sacrifice—giving up cherished ambitions, loved ones, or a great sum of money. But the underlying joy of the Lord made it all worthwhile. A will and life completely surrendered to the God of love will bring joy under all circumstances.

Christ Manifested

The next result of a surrendered life is Christ manifesting Himself to us. On the night in which Jesus was betrayed, He said to His disciples, *"He that hath my commandments, and keepeth them, he it is that loveth me: and he that loveth me shall be loved of my Father, and I will love him, and will manifest myself to him"* (John 14:21). Surrendering ourselves to Christ brings Christ to us.

It is true that the full manifestation of Jesus lies in that future glad day when *"the Lord himself shall descend from heaven with a shout, with the voice of the archangel, and with the trump of God"* (1 Thessalonians 4:16). But there is a manifestation of Jesus possible to us now, when the Son and the Father come to us and make their home with us (John 14:23).

You say you don't know what it means for Christ to manifest Himself to you. Have you yielded yourself to Him? Are you keeping His command-ments? Do not ask which com-mandment is great and which is small, which is important and which is unimportant, but only ask which commandment is His and keep that. If you are obeying His words, you will know what it is to have Him manifest Himself to you; your joy will be full.

You will be glad when you see the Lord.

We are told in one place, *"Then were the disciples glad, when they saw the Lord"* (John 20:20). You will be glad, also, when you see the Lord. And you will see Him when you go to Him and say, "I surrender my life completely to You. Please manifest Yourself to me according to Your promise."

Receive the Spirit

One more result of the surrendered will and life is revealed by Peter in Acts 5:32: *"The Holy Ghost, whom God hath given to them that obey him."* A surrendered will and life is the great key to receiving the Holy Spirit. Everything hinges on this. We may plead with God for the filling of the Holy Spirit, but unless we are yielded to Him to the very center of our beings, nothing is likely to come of it.

Perhaps He comes with great surging waves of power and joy; perhaps in a gentle calm that steals over our whole beings; perhaps in a still, small voice that whispers, *"If we ask any thing according to his will, he heareth us: and if we know that he hear us, whatsoever we ask, we know that we have the petitions that we desired of him"* (1 John 5:14–15).

Regardless of the way He comes, it is with power. The great secret of power for God is the Holy Spirit upon us (Acts 1:8). And the great secret of the Holy Spirit's coming upon us is a surrendered will, a yielded life. The Holy Spirit's power is so wondrous, so blessed, and so glorious! Would you like to have it? *"Yield yourselves unto God, as those that are alive from the dead, and your members as instruments of righteousness unto God"* (Romans 6:13).

> **The Lord always comes with power.**

Obtaining Power

We have seen in previous chapters the power of the Word of God, the power of the Holy Spirit, and the power of prayer. But the one great condition of obtaining this power in and through our lives and service is a surrendered will, lives given absolutely, unreservedly, and totally to God. Will you surrender to Him?

The Power of a Surrendered Life

How foolish it is not to! You are robbing yourself of everything that makes life really worth living and of the joy, beauty, and glory of eternity. Will you yield today?

About the Author
R. A. Torrey

About the Author

R. A. Torrey

Reuben Archer Torrey (1856–1928) was born in Hoboken, New Jersey, on January 28, 1856. He graduated from Yale University in 1875 and from Yale Divinity School in 1878.

Upon his graduation, R. A. Torrey became a Congregational minister. A few years later, he joined Dwight L. Moody in his evangelistic work in Chicago and became the pastor of the Chicago Avenue Church. He was selected by D. L. Moody to become the first dean of the Moody Bible Institute of Chicago. Under his direction, Moody Institute became a pattern for Bible institutes around the world.

Torrey is respected as one of the greatest evangelists of modern times. At the turn of the century, Torrey began his evangelistic tours and crusades. He spent the years of 1903–1905 in a worldwide revival campaign, along with the famous song leader Charles McCallon Alexander. Together they ministered in many parts of the world and reportedly brought nearly one hundred thousand souls to Jesus. Torrey continued worldwide crusades for the next fifteen years, eventually reaching Japan and China.

During those same years, he served as dean of the Bible Institute of Los Angeles and pastored the Church of the Open Door in that city.

Torrey longed for more Christian workers to take an active part in bringing the message of salvation through Christ to a lost and dying world. His straightforward style of evangelism has shown thousands of Christian workers how to become effective soulwinners.

R. A. Torrey died on October 26, 1928. He is well-remembered today for his inspiring devotional books on the Christian life, which have been translated into many different languages.